A SUITE OF ENGLISH FOLK SONGS

Rory Boyle

1. THE WRAGGLE TAGGLE GIPSIES

CH 55344

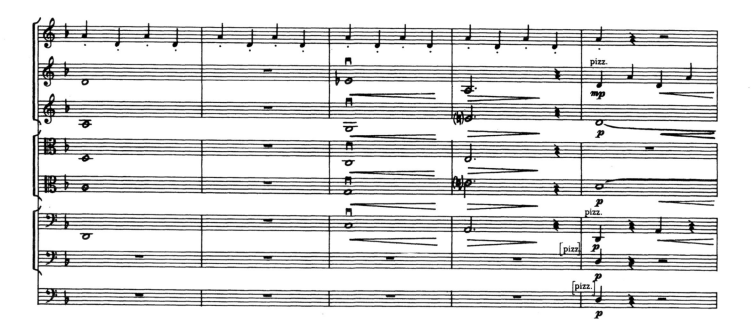

2. O WALY, WALY

3. BLOW AWAY THE MORNING DEW

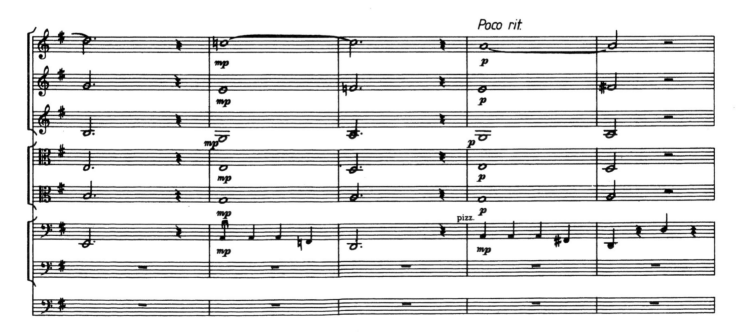

PLAYSTRINGS

MUSIC FOR
STRING ORCHESTRA

PLAYSTRINGS provides an enjoyable and varied repertoire for young string orchestras, carefully structured in two levels which offer music suitable for players of two terms' to two years' and one years' to three years' experience.

The **Easy** level does not normally exceed Grade 2 in difficulty, while the **Moderately Easy** level includes some parts of around Grade 3 standard. Most of the parts are playable in first position only. **PLAYSTRINGS** is thus an ideal introduction to orchestral playing for young string players.

Allowing for occasional variations, the pieces have the following instrumentation:

EASY	**MODERATELY EASY**
Violin 1	Violin 1
Violin 2	Violin 2
Violin 3 *(=Viola 2)*	Violin 3
Viola 1 *(optional)*	Viola
Viola 2 *(optional, = Violin 3)*	Cello
Cello 1	Double Bass
Cello 2 *(optional)*	
Double Bass *(optional)*	

Scores are issued separately for each title, and a set of parts contains sufficient material for an orchestra of around 30 players. Larger groups will find that two or more sets of parts added together will cater adequately for their needs.